VICTOR DOWD AND THE WORLD WAR II GHOST ARMY

Spy on History®

VICTOR DOWD AND THE WORLD WAR II GHOST ARMY

Written by Enigma Alberti
Illustrated by Scott Wegener

WORKMAN PUBLISHING
New York

Copyright © 2017 by Workman Publishing Co., Inc.

Text by Enigma Alberti

Illustrations by Scott Wegener

Library of Congress Cataloging-in-Publication Data is available.

ISBN 978-1-5235-0770-2

Workman books are available at special discounts when purchased in bulk for premiums and sales promotions as well as for fund-raising or educational use. Special editions or book excerpts can also be created to specification. For details, contact the Special Sales Director at the address below, or send an email to specialmarkets@workman.com.

Workman Publishing Co., Inc.
225 Varick Street
New York, NY 10014-4381
workman.com

WORKMAN and SPY ON HISTORY are registered trademarks of Workman Publishing Co., Inc.

Printed in China

First paperback printing February 2019

Originally published in hardcover in December 2017

10 9 8 7 6 5 4 3 2 1

This book tells a story of suspense and intrigue.

There's also a mystery *in the book itself.*

Use the spycraft tools in this envelope to decode clues and codes hidden throughout the book . . .

and find Victor's hidden sketchbook!

Sergeant Victor Dowd stepped out of the plane onto the metal mesh of the temporary runway.

Just beyond, he could see Omaha Beach.

Last week, it had been the site of the D-Day invasion. A huge wave of Allied soldiers had crossed the English Channel to France by plane, parachute, and every kind of boat you could imagine.

Their goal:

To take back
France from the
Nazis.

To push those Nazis back into Germany. And to defeat them once and for all.

Even though the invasion took place a week before, the beach was still full of people.

The sky was still FILLED with planes.

And the ocean was still full of ships, from big carriers to tiny landing craft.

As Vic glanced around at his new surroundings, he could also see the casualties. Wounded men lay on the runway, waiting to be airlifted to medical units. Beyond them, Vic could see the bodies of soldiers who had lost their lives on the beach. They were still waiting to be given a proper burial.

Until this minute, it had been hard for Vic to believe the war was real. He and his fellow platoon members had gone through tough training. They'd learned to march. They'd become experts at using their equipment.

But until today, they had only done drills.

Of course, Vic had known there was a war raging across the channel.

And he had felt eager to get to the front and join the fight.

But even though he had a vivid imagination, he could never have imagined the sights he was seeing now: tanks and trucks as far as the eye could see, the wounded lying in rows, the black smudges where shells had exploded.

Or the sounds. Even though the battle on Omaha Beach was over, German machine gun fire still rattled in the distance.

The ferocious German army had turned Europe upside down and threatened the peace and freedom of the whole world.

They were on the defensive now after the D-Day invasion, but they were hardly beat.

And some people thought they were the best army in the world.

"Sergeant!" someone called.

Vic turned around. A bag was flying toward him. He caught it just in time. It contained parts for the weapons he and his platoon had been ordered to use against the German army.

They weren't like the weapons used by the other armies in Europe.

Vic's platoon hadn't been issued their own machine guns or heavily armored tanks.

Instead, they had been ordered to fight the war with guns and tanks and planes made of inflatable rubber.

These fake weapons had been specially designed to fool the Germans into thinking there was a large, dangerous force in place, when in fact it was only Vic's platoon and their very big blow-up toys.

The army had assigned just over a thousand men to this secret deception unit, which had the code name "Blarney."

The members of Vic's platoon, the Fourth Platoon of Company D, led by Lieutenant Bernie

Mason, were the first to arrive in France.

Before the army sent the rest of the deception unit over, they wanted to see if this crazy idea of using blow-up tanks to fool the Germans would really work.

Vic's platoon's mission: to protect the first heavy-artillery battalion to land in France after D-Day. To do this, they were supposed to set up dummy guns a mile ahead of the artillery's actual line.

The objective: to draw German fire away from the real artillery and toward the fake.

In other words, Vic and his platoon would know their deception had worked if the Germans started shelling them.

The officers who dreamed up this secret deception unit called it the Twenty-Third Headquarters Special Troops.

The men who were in it called it the

Ghost Army.

It was a top-secret project—so secret that nobody told enlisted men like Vic everything that was really going on.

But during the few months before D-Day, when many of the members of the Ghost Army had trained together at an English country estate called Walton Hall, the men had put most of the pieces together.

Vic was part of the 603rd Engineer Camouflage Battalion Special. This was the largest division in the Ghost Army, with close to four hundred men.

Most of the men of the 603rd hadn't been recruited through the normal draft. Instead, they'd been handpicked for their skills in drawing and design from art schools all over the US, especially from Philadelphia and New York.

Vic, who was from Brooklyn, had gone to Pratt, a New York art school. He'd only been out of school for a few years and was working at a comics studio, drawing characters like Bulletman, Captain Midnight, and Spy Smasher, when the dean of his art school asked if Vic would consider joining a special unit of army artists.

Before they arrived in England, the 603rd had spent two years doing deception work. They'd helped develop and test the inflatable guns, planes, tanks, and vehicles that Vic's company was about to try out for the first time against the Germans. Some of Vic's unit had even camouflaged important military sites in the United States. They'd used their artistic talents to disguise bomber planes and coastal defenses so that spy planes couldn't see them.

When the men were training at Walton Hall, their leaders had told them that the Twenty-Third Headquarters Special Troops would be a kind of traveling show, putting on a performance for a very tough audience: the German army.

Vic's unit, the 603rd, would set the stage with their inflatables.

Then two other groups would step in: the signal company and the sonic unit.

The men of the Signal Company Special were top-notch radio operators. It was their job to imitate the radio transmissions of whatever unit the Ghost Army was ordered to impersonate.

Why?

So that the Germans who were listening in would believe there was a unit where the Ghost Army had set up camp. Then the real unit could move somewhere else, without the Germans knowing where they'd gone.

One of the things Allied forces had learned early in the war was that German spies were great at picking up Allied radio transmissions. Just by listening in on radio traffic, the Germans could guess, very accurately, where Allied troops were and what they were doing.

The GERMANS listened

so closely to Allied radio transmissions that they could tell one unit from another by their radio habits. The Germans knew how often different units sent messages. They knew what kinds of messages each unit sent. They knew the names and nicknames of men in the various units.

The Germans could even tell different Morse code operators apart, because every person tapped out code a little differently—the same way every person has different handwriting.

So if the radio operators in the Ghost Army wanted to convince the Germans that they were a real unit, they were going to need to copy that unit's radio habits perfectly.

And getting it right could be a matter of life or death, not just for the men of the Ghost Army but for the soldiers in other units whose lives they were assigned to protect.

To do all this, the signal company learned everything they could about the radio habits of the unit they had to imitate. They were so good at this that they could even mimic the different ways each radio operator tapped out Morse code.

The men of the sonic company were the other players in the Ghost Army's show. Officially known as the 3132 Signal Service Company Special, their job was sound effects.

They had spent the past months making recordings of trucks and men moving in, bridges being built, and orders being given—any sounds that would fool the enemy into thinking there was a big force somewhere even when there wasn't.

The sonic company had created an entire library of sounds, including tanks moving around, trucks starting up, and officers shouting. They kept them on miles of magnetized wire, because wire wouldn't skip when it played back, like a record did.

Depending on the illusion they wanted to create, the sonic company would mix different sounds from their library together. Then they would play them from giant speakers mounted on the backs of half-tracks, vehicles with wheels on the front and tank tracks on the back. The half-tracks were specially designed so that the speakers could fold into them and completely disappear. When one was on the move, it looked like just another regular piece of army equipment.

Most of the men in the sonic company had experience working with sound. But the sonic company also had several weathermen in the unit. Temperature and wind has a big effect on how sound travels, so they always had to take the weather into account.

One other unit was part of the Ghost Army, too. The 406th Engineer Combat Company Special included the only trained fighting soldiers in the group—not quite two hundred men out of the thousand total.

The combat engineers provided security, keeping snoopers away from Ghost Army deceptions. The last thing the Ghost Army wanted was to have a local civilian wander into one of their camps and realize they were armed with nothing more than a bunch of rubber tanks.

But the combat company also helped create the deceptions. They dug real tank and artillery positions for the phony dummies, and they set up real explosives to create flashes that made it look like the rubber guns could really fire.

All the men in the Ghost Army were handpicked and highly skilled.

But most of them had never been trained for combat.

The combat engineers had, but there were only enough of them to defend the unit, not to attack.

And almost no one in the Ghost Army had ever seen any action.

So in the Ghost Army, men like Vic were in a very strange position.

It was their job to get the Germans to shoot at them.

But they weren't equipped to shoot back.

((•~wwwwwwwwwwww~wwww ((•)) ~wwww~wwwwwwwwwww~•))

Vic and his platoon spent their first night in France in a foxhole with German artillery fire raining down all around them.

"I don't know how you did it," one of his buddies told Vic when he woke up the next morning. "You were the only one of us who got any sleep."

Before the platoon left Omaha Beach, Vic had time to make a quick sketch: a German "potato masher" hand grenade left lying on the ground next to an empty helmet.

From then on, there wasn't much time to draw.

Vic and his platoon had brought their inflatable dummies over to France with them. But the dummies were huge and heavy, and apparently nobody had thought to arrange any transport for them once they got to France.

So the first order of business was to scrounge transport for them and their gear.

Once they found a truck, they caught up with the artillery group they were assigned to imperson- ate, which had already moved inland from the beach.

Then Vic and the rest of his platoon swung into action.

About a mile from the real artillery line, they dug in positions for their inflatable guns. They covered the fake guns with real camo netting so that they appeared camouflaged but were still visible to enemy aircraft.

The combat company improvised flash canisters that went off when the real guns fired, to make it look like the shells came from the inflatables.

And then they all waited.

It was hard to believe that they could get the Germans to waste real shells on a bunch of rubber guns.

And it was a strange feeling to *hope* that the Germans would fire on them.

But then the first shell landed. And then another.

It was clear the Germans were aiming for them, and not for the soldiers behind them with real guns—the real artillery line.

That month, Vic's platoon moved into ten different sites with the artillery unit they were assigned to protect as they traveled up the French peninsula.

Again and again,

landed around GERMAN **shells** the dummy guns of the

GHOST ARMY—

and not the real guns farther back.

Again and again, Vic and his buddies scrambled for cover as shells fell around them.

But despite all those shells, the Ghost Army platoon made it through their first operation with no casualties.

It wasn't fun to be fired on, especially when they had no guns to shoot back. But even without fighting back, Vic's platoon had won a victory.

There was no question their first deception had fooled the Germans.

The crazy idea of using blow-up tanks and guns to trick the enemy had worked.

Most of the Ghost Army arrived in late June. When Vic and his platoon were released from their work with the artillery unit, they met up with the rest of their camouflage unit in the fields outside a small French town. The signal company was with them, too, but the sonic company was still over in England, putting the final touches on their sonic spoofs.

For several days, the camouflage company tested the new equipment they'd brought with them from England. They set up every single dummy to make sure they all still worked.

One day, two Frenchmen on bikes somehow managed to get through their top-secret security perimeter.

The first thing they saw was four American GIs picking up a forty-ton Sherman tank.

The bicyclists watched in shock, wondering how in the world four men could lift something so heavy.

"The Americans are very strong," one recruit told them as they were hustled away.

((•—wwwwwwwwww—www ((•)) —www—wwwwwwwww—•))

Now that most of the Ghost Army was assembled in France, it wasn't long before they got their first big assignment.

The mission of Operation Elephant was simple.

The Second Armored Division was moving up to the fighting line, but they wanted to keep that news secret from the Germans for as long as possible.

So the Ghost Army was assigned to make it seem like the armored division was still in place, far from the battle, even after they had started to move up for the fight.

The plan: As the armored division moved out, the Ghost Army would replace them with dummies,

setting up a
fake tank
or inflatable gun in the place of each real one.

From the beginning, the operation was a mess.

Orders weren't well coordinated. The real Second Armored moved out in broad daylight instead of under cover of night, and they used the main roads where anybody could see them.

If a German informant spotted the real Second Armored on the move, then the whole Ghost Army deception would be for nothing.

Not only that, it might make the Germans wonder why another unit was pretending to be the Second Armored. They might even realize that the Allies were using a top-secret deception unit.

But despite the mistakes,

the Ghost Army didn't give up.

They spent the next two days setting up a hundred inflatables, camouflage nets, and a dummy airstrip.

But they still had a lot to learn.

It was amazing how much they hadn't thought of.

For instance, sometime during the operation, someone realized that real tanks make tracks—unlike inflatable dummies. A tank that didn't make tracks was a dead giveaway.

So the Ghost Army combat unit started using their bulldozers to make tracks for the fake tanks.

"You know," someone else realized, "the same thing is true for our inflatable guns. If we were really using them, there would be artillery shells all over the place."

So the Ghost Army started piling spent artillery shells around their fake guns.

"And a lot of soldiers usually make a big mess," one man recognized. "They build a lot of fires. They hang out a lot of laundry."

So the Ghost Army started building fires, hanging out laundry, and spending as much time as possible outside so that it looked like there were even more men stationed inside, unseen.

In Vic's camouflage unit, they discussed how to make their camouflage convincing.

"A real unit would never park a tank without covering it with camouflage netting," they reasoned.

So Vic's company had to use camouflage nets, too, to look like a real unit.

But it turned out that Vic's camouflage group was a bit *too* good at camouflage.

They did such a good job of camouflaging their inflatable tanks and trucks that some of the inflatables were completely hidden. Friendly Allied pilots flew over the spot and couldn't see anything there.

The whole goal of the camouflage unit was for the Germans to catch sight of their fake equipment.

So Vic's company learned to thin out their camo mesh. Sitting around the camp, they pulled half of the fabric strips out of every net so that the tanks and guns would be visible.

To do their job, the camouflage experts had to get worse at camouflage.

Nobody was sure if the Ghost Army's first big deception had worked or not.

But they had certainly learned a lot.

The biggest lesson: They couldn't always follow the plans they'd been given. Because once they got close to the front line, things were always changing.

For one thing, the German air force, known as the Luftwaffe, was losing strength. They weren't flying nearly as many flights as they had earlier in the war.

So Vic's camouflage company realized they wouldn't be putting on their show for planes in the sky. They needed to fool people on the ground.

That wouldn't just involve dummies and camouflage nets. It would mean putting on a show that could convince anybody who came by that they were traveling with

far more men,

and far more

FIREPOWER,

than they actually had.

So Vic's company started to develop "poop sheets" for every unit they had to impersonate.

A poop sheet collected all the information that Vic and his fellow men could get on a unit so that they could create a convincing imitation. Poop sheets included the code names a unit used, the markings they put on their vehicles, how their signs were painted—even how their uniforms were worn.

Whenever the Ghost Army planned a deception in the future, they vowed, everyone would be briefed about the unit they were impersonating. They would know that unit's history and be able to talk about that unit's officers just as if they were in it.

But no matter how much new work they took on, the men of the Ghost Army still found a little time to make art.

Wherever they went, they drew and sketched and painted. Sometimes they used nothing more than ink and spit, and they worked on everything from notebooks to old receipts.

They drew each other. They also drew families who had been displaced by the war. Sadly, this was a common sight.

One day, they traveled to a nearby town, where the local children collected pieces of broken stained glass and asked the soldiers if they could trade the glass for some chocolate.

It was difficult to witness the destruction the German army had left behind in France.

But it also helped Vic and his buddies know what they were fighting for.

When their next order came,

they'd be ready.

((•~ᴡᴡᴡᴡᴡᴡᴡᴡᴡᴡᴡ~ᴡᴡ ((•)) ᴡᴡᴡ~ᴡᴡᴡᴡᴡᴡᴡᴡᴡᴡ~•))

In late July, seven weeks after the D-Day landing that had brought Vic to France, the Allies finally broke through German defenses.

General George Patton's Third Army was poised to sweep across France in a race to surround the German army—and defeat it.

But to do that, Patton needed the element of surprise.

So the Ghost Army was called into action.

Their mission: to make it look as if the Allies planned to head *west*, not east.

If the Ghost Army succeeded, the Germans would defend the wrong place.

And that meant the Germans would have less to throw at Patton when he struck.

In early August, the Ghost Army went to work.

They broke into four separate groups, each portraying a real army division.

But they all had one thing in common: All four of them headed west to confuse the German generals.

For days, the signal company men kept up a steady stream of fake radio messages in hopes that the Germans would intercept them and believe that real units were moving in.

Vic's division set up more than seventy inflatable tanks, and did everything else they could think of to make the Germans believe that there was a real military unit in the area.

They stenciled the bumpers of their trucks and jeeps with the markings of the division they were impersonating. They wandered around nearby towns wearing that division's patches.

If they couldn't get patches, no problem. There were so many artists in their ranks that someone could just paint a patch right onto a jacket.

Two members of the Ghost Army even got the bright idea to dress up like American military police. To give the impression that there was a real division in town, they went into a dozen local bars and announced to everyone that the Americans were heading out, so any GIs in the bar better get going.

By the end of the operation, the men had started to refer to all this set making and acting as "special effects."

It felt like putting on a play.

But they were playing on a deadly stage.

As usual, the Ghost Army only knew they had done their job when they got fired on.

They could tell that German fire increased after they put on a "show."

But they had another way to

tell that the Germans were "listening in" on their radio transmissions. The Germans had special transmitters designed to jam the radio signals and spoil the communications of nearby Allied troops, and they were using them to jam Ghost Army radios.

That meant the Germans were hearing their radio deceptions—and believed them.

It was a strange kind of applause to get.

But what mattered most to the Ghost Army was that the Germans stayed just where the Allies wanted them to long enough for Patton to surround them.

When the last Germans on the French coast realized they were defeated, they retreated in a panic.

Along the way, they abandoned all kinds of equipment.

Fifty thousand of them were captured.

The rest were on the run.

The Allies broke out of Normandy at last and began to

sweep across

FRANCE,

and the Ghost Army went with them.

By the end of August, only a handful of Germans were left in France.

But the ones who held the port of Brest, at the tip of the Brittany peninsula, were tough.

They'd been under siege for weeks, but they showed no signs of giving up.

So the Ghost Army was called in.

Their job this time: to impersonate an armored division so that the German general Ramcke would think he was facing more tanks than the Americans actually had.

If the plan worked, the Germans would move their antitank weapons and soldiers to their flanks to defend themselves against the Ghost Army's inflatable tanks.

Then it would be easier for the Allies to attack the Germans in Brest.

The Ghost Army's sonic company had finally arrived from England with their wire recordings of troops marching, generals shouting, trucks moving, and bridges being built.

This was the first time the Ghost Army would get to use all their deception tactics at once: visual, radio, and sonic.

Unfortunately, the weather didn't cooperate. Vic and his company traveled two days through the rain to get to Brest. And when they arrived: more rain.

But that didn't stop the sonic company from putting on their first show of the whole war.

As soon as they arrived, they drove their trucks right up to the German front line.

Then, when night fell, the sonic company set the stage just five hundred yards away from the German guns.

It was an eerie experience for Vic and his buddies to hear the disembodied sounds rolling through the darkness.

The sonic unit started by playing the sound of one tank approaching. Then the sound of another tank. Then, layering recording on top of recording, they played the sounds of a whole convoy of

tanks
and
heavy
trucks moving in.

They played the sounds of bushes crackling.

They played the sounds of gears shifting.

"No, no, no!" recorded voices called through the night. "Not here. Over there. That's right."

The sound was so realistic that it was hard for Vic to believe it wasn't real.

Through it all was the sound of the rain. It was all too real: cold and unrelenting.

As the rain poured down on them, Vic's company set up their dummy tanks, jeeps, and trucks.

"Hurry up," one soldier told another. "We've got a hundred of these to set up by morning."

"This one's done."

"You call that done? It's not even half-inflated."

"Are you kidding me? It was full a minute ago."

"These valves leak in the rain," someone else called over to them. "Just to make life more interesting."

"You're right," the first soldier said. "The gun on this tank is drooping all the way to the ground."

"We've got to get it right by morning. That's a dead giveaway."

((•─wwwwwwwwwww─wwww─ (((•))) ─wwww─wwwwwwwwwwww─•))

Soaked and tired, Vic's group was still up at first light to begin the "special effects."

They lit fires, pitched tents, and hung laundry to make it look like there were ten times more of them than there really were.

They switched the patches on their jackets.

They painted new markings on their trucks.

They drove the trucks back and forth to town.

That night, they got their first sign that the deception was working—when the Germans started to shell their phony position.

The Germans had moved dozens of antitank guns away from the actual fighting. They were using them now to shoot at a Ghost Army armed with nothing but sound and special effects.

So Vic and his company dug shelters in the ground to protect themselves from the German artillery barrage.

They knew that every shell falling around them was a small victory. The surrounded Germans were almost out of ammunition. That meant that every shot they made brought them closer to defeat.

And every shell they sent toward the Ghost Army's position was a shell that wouldn't land somewhere else to harm another Allied soldier.

As the Ghost Army held their position outside Brest, the Allies liberated Paris.

The German general who held Brest was tough. The Allies had hoped to force him to surrender early, but he held out for a month longer.

By that time, the Ghost Army had been ordered to new quarters in Saint-Germain, just twenty miles outside Paris.

The Parisians were still celebrating, and the mood in Vic's company was triumphant.

Sure, the Germans were still giving Patton a hard time in some places.

But

PARIS was free.

It was hard to believe the Germans could fight much longer. A lot of men in the Ghost Army figured the war might be over in a month.

None of them could wait to get home.

But in the meantime, they had Paris.

((•-ⱳⱳⱳⱳⱳⱳⱳⱳⱳⱳⱳⱳⱳ-ⱳⱳⱳ (((•))) -ⱳⱳⱳ-ⱳⱳⱳⱳⱳⱳⱳⱳ-•)))

Paris wasn't just the capital of France. Many people thought it was the world capital of art. It was full of architecture, fashion, museums—and women.

So the men of the Ghost Army went into Paris every chance they got.

Vic hitched his first ride into Paris in a sidecar attached to the motorcycle of an eccentric Englishman who had settled in Saint-Germain after the Great War, twenty years before.

Vic had seen pictures of the great avenue of the Champs-Elysées and the giant arch of the Arc de Triomphe. But pictures couldn't compare to the actual sight of them, growing closer and closer as he approached the city.

Those days after Paris was liberated were something special.

And so were the Parisian women. They wore bright clothes and had incredible hairdos, and they were intrigued by the men in uniform.

Some of Vic's buddies flipped frantically through their French-English dictionaries, trying to find just the right phrase to impress the women.

Others walked the streets alone, trying to process everything they'd seen during the war.

It was easy for the men to get to know the Parisians. The locals were eager for the cigarettes, chocolate, and cheese that the soldiers had with them.

And the Parisians provided Vic with inspiration. As soon as he arrived in Paris, he began sketching everyone he saw: women riding bikes, people in bars.

It was a relief to use his talent just to make a quick picture instead of using it to fool the Germans and bring enemy fire down on his own head.

But those magical days after the liberation of Paris couldn't last forever.

The war, it turned out, wasn't really over yet.

Not by a
long shot.

General Patton and his army swept across France at an incredible pace, driving out the Germans as they went.

In fact, at least one Ghost Army operation was canceled because Patton was moving so fast that no one could catch up to him.

But a few weeks after the liberation of Paris, Patton stopped to mass his troops for a new attack.

His goal this time: to dislodge the Germans from the French fortified city of Metz.

But there was a

problem.

Patton had moved so quickly across France that a

had opened in his line.

North of Metz, for an entire seventy miles, there were hardly any Allied forces. Just one single group of cavalry.

That single cavalry group would be no match for the German forces that faced Patton and his army if the Germans got wise to the gap.

And if the Germans stormed through that gap, they could easily surround Patton—and smash the Allied forces.

If that happened, there was no telling how much longer the war would drag on or who would win.

So until another real division could fill that seventy-mile gap, the Ghost Army was called in.

They had drawn German attention away from the real fighting in Brittany.

They had fooled the German general under siege at Brest.

But until now, they had always been in the background, supporting real troops.

They had never been called on to do anything like this: Impersonate an entire division in one of the most dangerous showdowns between the Allies and the Nazis.

And this time, they wouldn't just be protecting the lives of one other division.

The fate of Patton's whole army—and the course of the war—hung in the balance.

To the relief of Vic and his company, the plan only called for two and a half days of deception before a real unit would move in to relieve them.

That short time frame was key.

This time they'd be performing their "show" right on the front lines, and they knew from experience that Germans were excellent at discovering the identity of Allied units when they moved up to the front.

So once the Ghost Army joined the line themselves, all eyes would be on them.

Every shoulder patch, every camouflage net, every phony salute and radio broadcast would be under intense scrutiny.

The tiniest mistake could **alert** the **Germans** to the fact that the **Ghost Army** **weren't** who they pretended to be.

That would blow their cover as a deception unit, and the Germans would be on guard against any future deceptions for the rest of the war.

Even worse, it could prove deadly for the Ghost Army. Their radios and loudspeakers and camouflage wouldn't be much defense against an invading German army.

And if the German army was provoked to roll over the Ghost Army, the entire Allied force would be at risk.

The Ghost Army wasn't in an easy position.

But it was only for two and a half days.

They could fool the Germans that long, the men in Vic's company told themselves.

Just long enough for the real fighting division to arrive.

The Ghost Army pulled into Bettembourg, Luxembourg, just south of Luxembourg City, after two hundred and fifty miles of hard travel from their camp outside Paris.

Their mission was simple: to join the front line.

But that was made difficult by the fact that the gap in Patton's line was so big nobody could figure out where the front line *was*.

Before the Ghost Army could even move into position, they had to find the Germans.

When their scouts located the German lines, they realized the Germans were a lot closer than anyone would have liked—only about two miles from the Ghost Army's current position.

But nothing was going to stop the Ghost Army from doing what they came to do.

By three in the morning, the deception was underway.

First the sonic team went to work. Vic heard the sounds of vehicles cutting tracks through the forest, loudspeakers blaring, sergeants' voices yelling: "Put out that cigarette! Now!"

Even though Vic knew it was all a show, it sure sounded like a whole division was moving in. In fact, the sounds were so real that some men actually began to see tanks in the dark. But Vic knew all too well that they weren't a whole division and they didn't have a single real tank to fight with.

They were only a handful of men with a few good tricks.

Did they have what it takes to fool the Germans and hold the line?

((•~ⅿⅿⅿⅿⅿⅿⅿ~ⅿⅿ ((•)) ⅿⅿ~ⅿⅿⅿⅿⅿ~•))

The next morning, Vic was up again before dawn, sewing needle in hand. Someone had come through the day before, handing out patches for the Sixth Armored Division—the unit the Ghost Army was impersonating.

Vic sewed his patch to the shoulder of his uniform, which was starting to look a little ragged from switching out so many patches.

Then he went out to greet the day.

He wasn't working on much sleep, and neither was anyone else.

He and his company had spent most of the previous night wrestling their inflatables into place in the dark and setting the stage with spent shells and camo nets.

Now, as day broke, men roved among the inflatables, putting on the finishing touches.

One pair of men scrambled to reinflate a tank with a drooping gun.

"Who camouflaged this truck?" an officer bellowed, yanking at the netting to reveal the shine of the front window. "You couldn't see it at all!"

As soon as the sun was up, THE SHOW BEGAN.

All day, the Ghost Army put on a tense play, doing everything they could to imitate an actual infantry battalion.

They collected firewood and congregated around the fires.

They did laundry and hung it out.

"My mom would be so proud of me," one soldier joked. "I've washed this shirt twice since the last time I wore it."

"You actually washed yours?" his buddy said. "I just dunked mine in the river."

They posted signs along the main supply routes.

They set up military checkpoints, just like a real division would do, to control who came in and out of their area.

They set up a water point outside town, because no big army could survive for long without a lot of water. If it didn't seem like they were using enough, the locals might get suspicious about how many men were actually stationed there.

They also painted Sixth Armored Division markings on their trucks.

"Finally, they let us paint," one soldier said with satisfaction, admiring his work as a truck rolled in, just returned from town.

"Don't get too attached to your masterpiece," his buddy said, slapping a swath of army green paint over the neat stencil lettering they had applied just hours before.

"Hey, what's the big idea?" his friend asked.

"We're putting new markings on it," his buddy said, "and sending it back to town so they think it's a whole different truck."

Everyone in the Ghost Army had been briefed on the history of the Sixth Armored, and the men who were sent to town in the trucks had been told to use it.

They went into every bar and café in town and made sure everyone they talked to knew what unit they were with.

"There's no unit like the Sixth Armored," they'd proclaim over a beer.

"I've been over here with the Sixth Armored for a year," they'd tell the waitress.

"This is nothing," they'd tell a worried housewife on the street. "We're not even all here yet. Wait till tomorrow. There are three times as many of us moving in tonight."

In the meantime, the radio corps brought in all their transmitters, headsets, and codebooks. They set up three phony radio networks, faking the radio traffic of the Sixth Armored right down to the unique patterns of their telegraph operators.

Just across the Moselle River, the Germans watched and listened.

So did the local civilians.

The Ghost Army saw people taking notes as they rolled past. Some even photographed the Ghost Army vehicles.

But attention meant DANGER.

If even one civilian got the idea that their tanks were dummies, the whole game was over.

The army decided that the inflatables were too risky and told Vic's unit to pack away the tanks.

From now on, the deception would go on with just sound and special effects.

A few real tanks arrived that evening, and Vic and his company spent the whole night taking the inflatables down.

As they did, the sonic unit broadcast the arrival of even more men, trucks, and tanks.

The next morning, Vic and his men kept up their deception in town.

Since they were pretending more men had arrived overnight, they drew even more water from the water point near Bettembourg.

It was Sunday, so some men went to church in town, making sure no one could miss that they were with the Sixth Armored.

That afternoon, Ghost Army observers watching the German front line saw new enemy units moving into place.

"You see that?" one said. "They're sending more men to meet us. They think we're a threat. They think we're the real Sixth Armored."

"I'd feel more celebratory if that didn't mean we've now got even more German guns aimed at us," his buddy said.

But at least the deception was almost over.

All they had to do was hang on until the next day, when the real division would move into place and the Ghost Army could leave.

EXCEPT the real division didn't come.

The Eighty-Third Infantry Division had been assigned to take the place of the Ghost Army to fill the hole in Patton's line.

But they had been delayed.

In their place came two assault gun troops and a tank company, but these forces were hardly a match for the huge numbers of Germans across the river.

And those Germans were getting aggressive.

The next day, telephone wires laid by the radio company were found cut.

Shots were fired on men collecting water at the water point.

Ghost Army outposts reported Germans in the woods just outside camp.

The Ghost Army's small force of combat engineers mounted machine guns on their trucks and started to patrol the roads between the front lines, sometimes in full view of the Germans.

Vic and the other men in his company did everything they could think of to keep up the deception that they were members of a huge artillery division with thousands of men.

The radio operators kept up their phony transmissions. They checked in with headquarters. They reported on the movements of German troops. They cracked the same kinds of corny jokes the Sixth Armored radio operators were known to crack from time to time.

The sonic units broadcast sounds of bridge building and troop movement for four nights straight.

Vic knew that every moment the deception stretched on, the chances that they would be discovered only grew.

But he also knew they were the only Allied soldiers who stood between Patton and the hostile German army.

Finally, seven days after the Ghost Army took up their position in Patton's line, the Eighty-Third Infantry arrived.

The deception had lasted almost three times as long as planned, and it had only grown more perilous with each passing day. German patrols had increased in the area since the Ghost Army arrived—which also increased the chance that the Germans would see through the deception.

But the Ghost Army had been successful. While they held the line, the Germans had moved two whole infantry divisions across the river, which took some pressure off Allied troops in the south.

Most important, the Ghost Army had kept the whole German army from recognizing that they stood just across the river from a gap of seventy unprotected miles.

With not much more than radios, paint, and imagination, the Ghost Army had held the Allied line.

As Vic and his company drove into Luxembourg City at the end of September, the streets were lined with cheering crowds waving American flags.

The city had just been liberated, and its people were ready to celebrate.

Vic's camouflage company was given an old seminary as barracks.

The Germans who had been there before had taken out all the furniture, but that wasn't what bothered the artists of the Ghost Army the most. What really drove them nuts was the terrible art the Germans had left behind: Nazi murals painted all over the walls.

But despite their lodgings, the men found a warm welcome in Luxembourg City. While the town hadn't escaped the war unscathed—the church had been bombed and lay in disrepair—it had survived and the people were friendly. And Vic wasn't the only man in the division who was glad to discover the local art supply stores.

The Ghost Army's deception work was far from over, however.

All that fall, using Luxembourg City as a base, they put on show after show.

((•~ww\/\/\/\/\/\~•(((•))) ~ww\/\/\/\/\/\~•)))

The Allied army was at a standstill on the German border for all of October, planning their next assault. But when the Allies went on the move again in November, the Ghost Army was at the heart of the action.

Heavy artillery guns were often the first clue the enemy got about where an army planned to attack. Before big guns could be used, they had to be hauled into place.

That gave enemy generals a very good idea of where an attack might come from. And if they knew that, they had a chance to prepare their defenses.

Unless they were fooled by the phony artillery of the Ghost Army.

As a key part of the new Allied offensive, the Ghost Army worked overtime, creating fake artillery units so that the real ones could move into place and launch surprise attacks.

But that wasn't the Ghost Army's only trick. They also broadcast radio and created special effects to make it seem as if infantry divisions were retreating to rest—when in fact they were moving up into the front lines.

This close to the action, Vic and his company were always under fire.

They dug their foxholes deep.

But **nobody** knew where the next **SHELL** would fall or **who** might get **HIT.**

For Thanksgiving, the men got an early Christmas present.

The movie star Marlene Dietrich arrived to sing for them. Lieutenant Bernie Mason, who led Vic's platoon, was the lucky guy who got to introduce her to the audience.

They even had real turkey for dinner.

But in Luxembourg City, the mood was growing tense.

Shots rang out every night.

There were still people in the city who were loyal to the Germans.

No one was sure who to trust.

Up at the German line, the Allies had launched an all-out attack, fighting a bloody advance through the Hürtgen Forest.

But south of the main battle, a thin spot had opened in the Allied line.

When the Ghost Army had held the line for Patton, nobody had been sure if the deception would work.

But by now, they were old hands at this.

They swung into action just north of Luxembourg City, imitating the Seventy-Fifth Infantry Division with every trick in their book.

They ran fake convoys up near the front line.

They broadcast the sounds of troop movements.

They set up radio networks.

They created a water point.

They posted military police checkpoints.

Harry Reeder, the commander of the whole Ghost Army, even put on fake general's stars and made a phony visit to their phony command center.

But this time it was the Ghost Army's turn to be surprised.

It turned out that the Allied commanders weren't the

only ones who had noticed that the area was thinly held.

The Nazis had seen the opportunity, too.

The Ghost Army had been trying to attract German forces to the area.

But more German forces than they had ever dreamed of were moving in.

The Nazis had amassed a huge force to launch their own surprise attack through the Ardennes—exactly where the men of the Ghost Army were stationed.

The Ghost Army now stood directly in the enemy's path.

As shells began to fall through the trees and gunfire rang through the woods, the Ghost Army fell back and returned to their quarters in Luxembourg City.

There they prepared for a full-scale retreat.

Vic and his division were given orders to set explosive charges on the vehicles that carried their equipment and inflatables. They didn't want the Germans to learn their deception secrets—even if it meant destroying their tools.

As German planes flew overhead, strafing the city below, men from the Ghost Army scrambled up to the roof of the seminary, where they set up a machine gun nest.

All night long, members of the Ghost Army took turns shooting back at the German planes.

It was the first and last time any of them would get a chance to take an actual shot at the enemy.

After all the time they had spent under enemy fire with no way to fight back, it felt good to take a shot.

But no matter how much fight the Allies put up, either on that seminary roof or on the front lines, the Nazis' surprise attack was too strong to match.

A few days later, nobody could deny that the Allied line

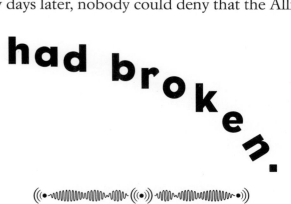

had broken.

In the Ardennes forest, Allied forces were in chaos.

As the front line collapsed, most of the American troops headed west toward Luxembourg City.

Suddenly the streets were flooded with retreating troops.

To make room for them, the Ghost Army was ordered to fall back.

Leaving Luxembourg, their home base for months, was tough.

Heavy December snow poured down as the Ghost Army moved out.

Vic watched as Luxembourgers replaced the American flags in their windows with white flags of surrender, or even Nazi swastikas.

Just weeks before, he and the other men had thought the war was almost over.

Now, nobody knew when the fighting would ever stop.

Or who would be the victor when it did.

((•—wwwVVVVVw—((•))—wwwVVVVw—•))

Less than a week later, it was Christmas.

Vic couldn't help thinking back to Christmases when he was a kid in Brooklyn.

In New York, the streets were hung with lights. Men sold Christmas trees from the sidewalk while crowds of happy shoppers walked by. Vic fondly remembered getting a nickel from his parents and buying a bag of roasted chestnuts from a holiday stand.

This Christmas could hardly be more different.

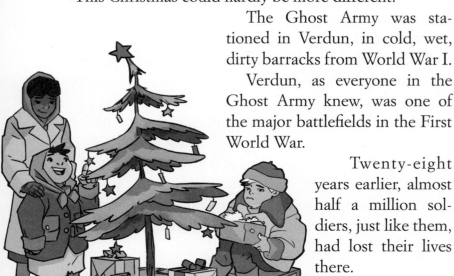

The Ghost Army was stationed in Verdun, in cold, wet, dirty barracks from World War I.

Verdun, as everyone in the Ghost Army knew, was one of the major battlefields in the First World War.

Twenty-eight years earlier, almost half a million soldiers, just like them, had lost their lives there.

In the window of one of the barracks, a skull sat unburied, helmet still on.

It wasn't exactly a cheerful Christmas decoration.

And this winter was the coldest France had seen in forty years.

Still, Vic and his company tried to celebrate.

The Ghost Army decorated a Christmas tree with garlands of paper and stars cut from tin cans, and they threw a party for the refugee children who were also taking shelter in Verdun.

As bad as the men had it, they knew these children had it worse.

The men of the Ghost Army still had their own families waiting for them back in the United States.

But many of these children had lost both their mothers and their fathers.

So the men of the Ghost Army put together dozens of boxes for the children and filled them with goodies from their own rations: candy, gum, and other food.

As he passed the presents out, Vic couldn't help noticing a little boy with incredibly sad eyes. The boy had opened his box to see the treats hidden inside. But still the boy didn't smile.

God knows what he's been through, Vic thought.

But if the Allies couldn't turn the tide of the war, Vic knew, all of them would have even bigger problems.

If they didn't stop the Nazis, what other tragedies would the world have to face in the New Year?

Maybe Christmas gave the Allies new courage, or maybe they were just sick of being tied down in the snow.

Whatever the reason, the tide began to turn. The day after Christmas, Patton broke through German forces around Bastogne. He and his army linked up with the 101st Airborne Division.

The Allies were on the offensive again, pushing the German army back.

And before New Year's Eve, the men of the Ghost Army were called into action.

They covered an infantry unit as it moved up to the front, using a whole host of "special effects": fake road signs, unit insignia, and the old water point trick.

The freezing cold of the winter posed a whole new challenge, however.

"I thought it was hard to get one of these things inflated in the rain," one man complained. "Then I saw how bad they behave in winter. Both armies might freeze to death before this war ends."

"It'll work," Vic told him. "It just takes longer."

"A *lot* longer," another man added.

"Great," the first one said. "We'll just have the signal company radio let the Germans know we'll be ready for them sometime in June."

And it wasn't just the inflatables that didn't work in the cold.

"This paint's made of oil," one of the men complained, squashing a clumped-up brush to the stencil he was using to change the markings on a jeep. "It shouldn't be freezing."

"Everything freezes when it gets cold enough," another soldier pointed out.

"Take your time," their commanding officer said. "Don't think of it as regular paint. Think of it as a new medium you're trying out."

"Yeah, ice paint," one of the soldiers said sarcastically.

"Hey, that sounds pretty good," the other one said. "Ice Paint. Maybe that will be the title of my first gallery exhibit, once we get out of all this."

Despite the new challenges of winter, their deception worked.

Once the real infantry unit had safely moved up into the front lines, Patton had a new task for the Ghost Army. He wanted to remove a veteran unit for some rest and bring a fresh one up, but the fresh unit was delayed.

So the Ghost Army was sent in to impersonate the veteran unit until the new one showed up.

Vic and his company played the parts of a field artillery battalion. They stenciled insignia on their helmets. They sewed on a new set of division patches. They put on the combat scarves the men of the real unit wore.

They even displayed German souvenirs on their trucks, to make it look like they were a hardened combat unit that had captured German helmets and flags in the heat of battle.

Then, when the fresh unit slipped safely into place,

the **Ghost Army** faded away as if they had never **been there.**

Through the heart of that winter, the Ghost Army staged deceptions every few days.

Their base camp now was at Briey, in another gloomy French military barracks.

From there, they traveled all over France to protect Allied forces and confuse the Germans as Patton moved his troops into place.

But the Ghost Army also made time to paint and draw.

Keith Williams, a member of Vic's camouflage outfit, was even known to do watercolors while he was on guard duty. He used a brush made out of a few tiny hairs and three buttons of watercolor paint stuck on his watch.

The men took turns hanging their creations in the attic above their quarters at Briey, turning the space into an art gallery.

They enjoyed each other's work, and the gallery offered a respite from battle. Stepping into the gallery felt like stepping into another place—a place far beyond the war.

All the while, the Allies continued their offensive. Slowly but surely, they pushed the Germans out of France, back across the Rhine River into Germany.

In early March, Allied troops captured a bridge on the Rhine and sent a handful of forces across, into the German heartland.

But everyone knew this was only the first step.

To win the war, the Allies would need to win a decisive victory in Germany—on the other side of the Rhine.

In the dead of night, Vic and his unit worked overtime setting up dummy tanks. Around them, through the darkness, the sonic team broadcast the sounds of phantom men and machines moving into position.

The goal: to pretend they were an infantry division preparing for battle outside the German town of Saarlautern.

That would give the real infantry division time to get into place for the attack they were planning farther north.

The Ghost Army had done it all so many times before that they could practically work with their eyes closed.

But this operation
was
DIFFERENT.

They were working incredibly close to the German front lines, so close that a German who took a good look at one of their inflatables might be able to tell it wasn't real.

And in that case, the Ghost Army's deception would be discovered.

So Vic and his company were relieved the next day when they got word that the operation was finished. They packed up their gear and piled into a truck, ready to move out.

Vic was sitting in the front of the truck, next to the driver, when the first shell hit.

The ground in front of them shook. It felt like an earthquake.

The next shell flew over their heads and hit the truck behind them. Pieces of metal flew in every direction, hissing through the air.

As Vic's ears rang, his mind raced.

Do I tell the men to get out of here now? he wondered.

Should he make a call on his own?

Should he wait for orders?

Just then, the radio crackled to life with the signal they had been waiting for.

It was time to move.

No one had to tell them twice.

But not everybody made it out alive.

One member of the Ghost Army, a sergeant just like Vic, was killed when his truck was hit by shrapnel. Another man, a captain, died when his jeep was shelled.

Fifteen other men were wounded.

Some of them lost limbs.

These were the worst casualties the Ghost Army had suffered since the deception unit was formed.

And the big crossing over the Rhine, where everyone knew they would face the fiercest German resistance yet, was still to come.

((•⁃ᴡᴡᴡᴡᴡᴡᴡ⁃((•))⁃ᴡᴡᴡᴡᴡᴡᴡᴡ⁃•))

Just days after the artillery attack, the Ghost Army learned what part they would play in the Rhine crossing.

A big one, it turned out.

General Dwight D. Eisenhower, the Allies' top American commander, planned to attack across the river on March 24.

One whole wing of his attack would be led by the American Ninth Army.

But Eisenhower wanted the Ghost Army to move into place on the banks of the Rhine a week *before* the real attack.

He wanted them to move up to face the German front lines, on their own, before any of the other Allied forces got there.

Their job: to convince the Germans that the Allied attack was going to come ten miles south of where Eisenhower had really planned it.

If the Germans didn't know where the attack was really coming from, they wouldn't be able to defend themselves.

And if the Germans didn't mount a tough defense, thousands of Allied lives would be saved and the Allied invasion might finally end the war.

But to complete the assignment, the Ghost Army would need to put on

the BIGGEST

deception

they'd ever attempted.

They weren't just pretending to be one unit this time. Or even one division.

They were pretending to be two separate divisions of the Ninth Army: the Thirtieth and the Seventy-Ninth. Those two divisions together included thirty thousand men.

There were just over a thousand in the Ghost Army.

To pull off this deception, every man in the Ghost Army would have to create the impression that there were twenty-nine more of him, all poised to attack.

And they'd have to do it on the front lines, just across the river from the German army.

Everything had to be perfect.

That included perfect cooperation with the real divisions the Ghost Army had to imitate.

As the real divisions headed north to where Eisenhower was massing troops for the attack, their radio operators

all went silent. They had planned this moment in advance with the radio operators of the Ghost Army.

At just that moment, Ghost Army radio operators began to broadcast, imitating the sounds of the departing troops.

To protect the real division, the broadcasts by the Ghost Army made it sound as if those troops were moving south, not north.

To do this, the Ghost Army radio operators had to be on the move themselves.

One Ghost Army broadcaster transmitted thirty messages from eight different locations that first day to give the illusion that he was part of a division moving into the front line.

EVERY detail had to be PERFECT.

Ghost Army radio operators even made sure they were broadcasting with the same amount of power as the radios they were replacing. They held a pencil to the antennae of the real division radio to see how big a spark it made. Then they turned the dials on their own radio set until it made the same size spark.

In the meantime, Vic's camouflage unit was hard at work.

Near the town of Krefeld, on the Rhine, they set off smoke screen after smoke screen, sending giant clouds billowing across the fields.

Real army units sometimes set off smoke screens to make it harder for the Germans to see their numbers and equipment. But for the Ghost Army, smoke screens were a great deception tool. Because the Germans had gotten used to the idea that there were usually soldiers hiding behind the smoke, the Ghost Army could trick the Germans into believing there were thousands upon thousands of soldiers moving in.

They created phony supply dumps, stacks and stacks of boxes and barrels that didn't really contain any supplies.

They set up fake headquarters and filled them with soldiers dressed up as commanding officers.

Because the Luftwaffe had been so damaged in the previous years of the war, the Ghost Army hadn't dealt with much air surveillance before. But now, in the final days of the war, the Germans threw everything they still had at the Allies. This meant that surveillance planes passed overhead constantly.

So Vic and his company were putting on a show this time not just for civilians on the ground but for spies overhead.

The camouflage company inflated almost every decoy tank and vehicle they had. They set them up in the forest, in the fields, and in the courtyards of buildings. When the men were finished, two hundred inflatable vehicles were scattered around two small towns just west of the Rhine, more than had ever been set up before.

Not only that, but the Allied command had ordered real tanks and guns to join the Ghost Army to help fool the Germans.

With one real tank parked just outside a forest, it was harder for the enemy to tell that the dummy tanks hidden just under the trees weren't real.

When the Ghost Army was given a few real antiaircraft guns, they set them up alongside eighty dummy guns.

It looked like they were preparing for a huge battle.

They even set up two fake airfields, with inflatable observation planes on the "runways."

At night, the sonic company broadcast the sounds of trucks rolling in to prepare for battle. During the day, they played the sounds of pontoon bridges being built across the river: hammered metal, shouted orders, splashing water.

A real bridging unit even joined the Ghost Army and started to build an actual bridge across the Rhine to support the deception.

But all the fake tanks and bridges in the world wouldn't fool the enemy if there were no soldiers camped nearby.

So real infantry divisions joined the Ghost Army, too. They camped all around the phony attack site, drove their trucks through town, and pretended to man the phony tanks and guns.

The Ninth Army supported the Ghost Army with real firepower, too.

To make it look like the dummy guns were real, the Ninth Army increased their artillery fire from the area, to give the Germans the idea that this was just a little taste of the coming attack.

Ninth Army reconnaissance planes flew mission after mission over the fake attack zone, to create the impression that they were gathering intelligence for the big battle.

The Ninth Army even set up field hospitals around the positions the Ghost Army had taken, to make it look like they were preparing to deal with the casualties of the coming fight.

The people in the nearby riverside towns were clearly convinced. Wherever Vic and his men went, they saw white flags on every door: a sign that people hoped would save their homes—or maybe even their lives—from destruction.

The Ghost Army even managed to fool at least one pilot on their own side. In the days leading up to the invasion, an Allied plane landed on one of the Ghost Army's fake runways, thinking it was the real thing.

But the local people and the confused pilot weren't the Ghost Army's real audience.

They were performing this whole show for the Germans across the Rhine.

Had it WORKED?

Did the Germans believe what they were seeing?

Were they on the other side of the river preparing for battle, too?

Or would they put up a deadly resistance ten miles north, where the real force of the Ninth Army was preparing their sneak attack?

There was only

ONE

WAY

to find out.

(((•∿∿∿∿∿∿ ((•)) ∿∿∿∿∿∿•)))

The night before the Allied invasion, Allied leaders gathered near the river.

Early the next morning, the order went out: It was time to cross the Rhine.

On the banks, the soldiers steeled themselves for fierce combat.

They hoped this would be the last battle of the war, but no one expected it to be easy.

If the Allies had learned anything about the Germans during this war, it was that they wouldn't give up without a tough fight.

One by one, group by group, Allied soldiers began to cross the Rhine.

They marched across pontoon bridges.

They stood on the decks of navy landing craft.

They held their breath and scanned the opposite banks.

Every single one of them was waiting for the fierce blast of German opposition they expected to rain down on them: bursting shells and screaming bullets that would leave wounds and steal lives and blow their bridges and ships to pieces.

But nothing happened.

When the Ninth Army got to the other side of the Rhine, the few Germans they found there seemed surprised—as if they were expecting the attack to come somewhere else.

The Allies had expected fierce German fighters.

They found feeble, disorganized troops.

Thousands of Allied soldiers streamed into Germany that day.

Allied leaders had feared they might suffer as many as ten thousand casualties in the crossing. Instead, fewer than fifty lives were lost.

The final crossing into Germany had cost fewer lives than some training exercises. And in the battle that followed, the Allies learned one reason why.

Captured German documents let Allied leaders see what plans the Germans had made in the days before the invasion. And those documents showed that the Germans believed the bulk of the Ninth Army was ten miles south of the real crossing—right where the Ghost Army had staged the deception.

With the crossing of the Rhine, the war in Europe was soon over.

Allied forces raced across Germany so quickly that there was no more need for deception, so the Ghost Army was assigned to guard camps full of people who had been forced from their homes by the war.

There were thousands of them from dozens of countries.

Vic and his buddies couldn't wait to get home. But these people didn't even know if they still had homes to go back to.

So while they were all waiting, Vic began to sketch.

He asked one person to sit for him, and the next thing he knew, three or four more were waiting to have their portraits drawn, too.

Proud young men and tired old men. Worried old women and young women in beautiful clothes. Sometimes Vic would sketch dozens of them in a single day.

His buddies sketched, too.

When each portrait was done, Vic and his fellow artists had the people add their signature to the art—a symbol that,

no matter

what **had happened**

to them in the war,

they **had made** **it through.**

These were the people the Ghost Army had been fighting for.

And now that the war was over, these were the people who would build the new world together.

Can you decipher
Vic's letter to find out
where he left
his sketchbook?

G_K N_G_W_F_T_,
M U R   Z   I

Q_   E_V_   O_D_   H_   L_Q_W_   M_   B_E_ S_O_ Y_F_T_A_
N I   O Y   S I   S O V   P K   U I   B Y D Z A N A P T

D_   H_ K_G_   L_B_T_   _ K_S_Z_   J_   J_N_ M_ Z_G_ _.
G I   N O X   P H Y   N Q L C H   M S   W G I G L B Z F Y L

S_V_'   D_Y_V_R_   _P_E_   J_ B_   T_L_U_   P_M_   F_H_X_
Z L ' J   C O   E X   G D   Z I V   C   D B   K U   Y

D_ V_J_ F_   _B_   O_Y_Q_   Y_U_L_H_ L_B_   O_K_   P_F_T_
U V   X I D   H T   S U F   Q   E Q B G B F S   D C   C

_O_ X_O_ _ M_   W_R_O_ N_Y_.   F_O_   U_   N_L_R_M_Z_
U X P B H V - A T G   B B   V K U   T U Y   D R E   X   A U

R_   C_   S_   H_E_ D_   D_   X_U_   _ T_ K_X_?
A P   E Y   V R   W O X J   A I U   R W I   Z R Y

HUA
XXX

Historical Note

The members of the Ghost Army were chosen because they were all great at telling stories: with sound, paint, or drama.

But they were also good at keeping a secret.

And because the Ghost Army wasn't declassified until 1996, many of them kept the secret of their exploits during the war for most of their lives.

Once the secret was out, though, an amazing story unfolded—both in declassified government documents and in the recollections, stories, and sketches of the men of the Ghost Army.

So all the details in this story are true. The Ghost Army really went to all the places they go in this book, and they really pulled off all the deceptions in this story. Even the thoughts and feelings of Victor and his fellow artists and soldiers are based in fact, drawn from their interviews, writings, and letters.

Victor didn't win the war alone. He represents all the men who risked their lives as part of the Ghost Army.

None of them could have done it on their own. But together they accomplished something that even the greatest artist might not have been able to imagine.

Bibliography

Beyer, Rick, and Elizabeth Sales. *The Ghost Army of World War II: How One Top-Secret Unit Deceived the Enemy with Inflatable Tanks, Sound Effects, and Other Audacious Fakery.* Princeton: Princeton Architectural Press, 2015.

Beyer, Rick. *The Ghost Army* (documentary). Plate of Peas Productions, 2013.

Gawne, Jonathan. *Ghosts of the ETO: American Tactical Deception Units in the European Theater, 1944–1945.* Philadephia: Casemate, 2014.

Holt, Thaddeus. *The Deceivers: Allied Military Deception in the Second World War.* New York: Skyhorse, 2010.

Kneece, Jack. *Ghost Army of World War II.* New Orleans: Pelican Publishing, 2001.

WAIT!

Have you figured out where Victor left his sketchbook?

Don't crack this seal until you've solved the mystery!

Answer Key

Map: The Morse code along the top and left borders of the inset map says "The sketchbook is in one of these locations." The code on the bottom of the map says "It's not H," meaning it is not in Briey.

Copyright page: The black letters spell out "Attention, spy—two false letters gain one true." This is a hint that you can decode many of the cryptograms throughout the book by aligning two letters on the cipher wheel included in the spy envelope. The red acetate (also included in the spy envelope) makes it easier to see the black letters.

Page 10: The fleur-de-lis symbol in the middle of the page references the Omaha Beach icon on the map. The words "Not Here" are hidden in the illustration to the right of Victor's head, meaning the sketchbook is not at Omaha Beach.

Page 13: Use the white vellum sheet with the rectangular cutouts (included in the spy envelope) to decode this clue. Place the vellum so that the insignia of the Ghost Army aligns with the illustration in the bottom right corner of the page. The die-cut window highlights the word "Blarney." The rest of this clue will be found by aligning the other insignias on the vellum with the matching insignias found on pages 17, 30, and 42. (The complete clue is: "The code is Blarney." This is the key to filling in the gaps in Victor's letter at the end of the book.)

Page 17: Place the vellum so that the insignia of the Ninetieth Infantry Division aligns with the illustration on the page. The die-cut window highlights the word "code." In the illustration of the radio operator, the dial is set on the letter F, which hints that Luxembourg may be an important location.

Page 18: The illustration of the tank contains several clues. The word "Blarney" is the key to Victor's final letter and is written on the side of the tank. The number 75 is printed twice on the tank, hinting at Luxembourg (the Ghost Army impersonated the Seventy-Fifth at Luxembourg). The set of letters along the bumper can be deciphered with the cipher wheel.

How to Use The Cipher Wheel: The cipher, which is a replica of the Diana Cryptosystem Cipher, is used to crack codes throughout this book. When you see one letter above another, it indicates that you must properly align the cipher to decode the message. For example, the first part of the message hidden in the illustration on page 18 is Q over W. To decode this, turn the inner wheel on the cipher so that Q is over W. The letter revealed in the cipher's cutout window is N. This means the hidden message begins with

N. Continue to decode the other letters in this way to get the message: "Not Briey," which means the sketchbook is not in Briey.

Page 20: The illustration of the helmet has Morse code that says "No" above the image of the fox. Since the fox is the symbol of Bouzonville on the map, this means that the sketchbook is not there.

Page 22: The illustration hides the words "It's not C," meaning the sketchbook is not in Brittany, which is marked with a C on the map.

Page 25: The Morse code along the side of the tank tracks says "Not Metz," meaning the sketchbook is not there.

Page 27: The frame around this page holds a special pattern that reveals a word if you look at it from an angle. The word is "Blarney."

Page 30: Place the sheet of vellum so that the insignia aligns with the matching illustration on the page. The die-cut window highlights the word "the."

Page 31: Place the red acetate over the radio to reveal an image of a unicorn and "not G." This indicates that the sketchbook is not in Metz.

Page 32: The letters on the bumper can be deciphered with the wheel and read "Follow the maze." This is a hint that the sketchbook is under the labyrinth on page 52. To emphasize this idea, there is an image of the labyrinth by the paint cans.

Page 34: The section-break icon of radio waves has a phrase written backward in cursive: "It's not I," meaning the sketchbook is not in Bouzonville, which is marked with an I on the map.

Page 39: Place the red acetate over the illustration to reveal the phrase "It's not A or J," meaning the sketchbook is not on Omaha Beach or in Dülken.

Page 42: Place the sheet of vellum so that the insignia aligns with the illustration on the page. The die-cut window highlights the word "is."

Page 47: The illustration of the elephant—which is associated with the Normandy location on the map—is coupled with the words "Kein Elefant," meaning "not elephant" in German. So the sketchbook is not in Normandy. Through the window, you can see the damaged church (the real location of the sketchbook).

Page 48: The frame around this page is a special pattern that reveals a phrase if you look at it from an angle. The phrase is "Not B or D," meaning the sketchbook is not in Normandy or Brest.

Page 52: The illustration features a lion in the foreground to indicate that this is Luxembourg. The church roof is destroyed, and the labyrinth that has been referenced throughout the book can be seen on the church floor. This is the location of the sketchbook!

Page 58: In the illustration, one gift box is labeled F-75. The letter F hints at the Luxembourg location on the map, while the 75 also hints at Luxembourg (the Ghost Army imitated the Seventy-Fifth Infantry Division while based in Luxembourg). On another gift, the image of the griffin is crossed out, meaning the sketchbook is not in Bettembourg.

Page 63: A couple of the arm patches in the illustration show instances of the number 75 to hint at Luxembourg. If you place the red acetate over the red parts of the illustration, you can see the phrase "Not in" and the symbol for Briey, meaning the sketchbook is not there.

Page 66: Place the red acetate over the illustration to reveal the phrase "It's not" and the symbol for Brittany, meaning the sketchbook is not there.

Page 69: On the helmet in the illustration, the backward E is crossed out, meaning the sketchbook is not in Bettembourg.

Page 71: The image at the edge of the page can be held up to a mirror to reveal the Brest symbol with an X crossing it out, meaning the sketchbook is not there.

Page 72: The border around this page is a special pattern that reveals a phrase if you look at it from an angle. The phrase is "Not Dülken," meaning the sketchbook is not there.

Page 75: The image at the edge of the page can be held up to a mirror to reveal the Dülken symbol with an X crossing it out—another clue that the sketchbook is not there.

Page 79: The initials of the soldiers in the illustration form a code that can be translated with the cipher wheel to spell out "BLARNEYBL." This is a hint that you must repeat the word "Blarney" when you are decoding Victor's letter.

Page 82: If you fill the gaps in Victor's letter with the word "Blarney" repeated, then you get everything you need to decode the letter with the cipher wheel. The decoded letter is revealed on the facing page.

Poop Sheet: The poop sheet includes a key to the Morse code used throughout this book. If you look at the back of the sheet, several letters appear to have bled through from the front. The letters spell out "In the church, under the labyrinth," to indicate the precise location of the sketchbook in Luxembourg.

HEY BUDDY,
GBK NGWFT,
MUR LZARI'

WE HAD TO GET OUT OF LUXEMBOURG
QN EVY OD BHL LQW RM BEESOYYFTA
NI OEY SI SOV APK UI NBYDZANAPT

SO FAST THAT I LEFT MY SKETCHBOOK.
BD HLKG RLBT E YKSZ BJ LJNAMRZGNE
GI NOXA PHYN N QLCH MS WGIGLBZFYL

IT'S UNDER THE RED TILE AT THE
SV'Y DYVRL APE JNB ETLU PM FHX
ZL'J COBEX GDR ZIV CYDB KU BLY

CENTER OF THE LABYRINTH IN THE
DAVJNF EB OYQ YYULHLLBA OK PFT
UVRXID HT SUF QBEQBGBFS DC RNC

BOMBED-OUT CHURCH. CAN YOU BRING
EOYXOB-LMA WRONNY EFO YUB NLRMZ
UXPBHV-ATG BBRVKU TUY DRE LXAAU

IT TO ME WHEN YOU COME HERE?
RR CN SE HEYD BDL XURN TEKX
AP EY VR WOXJ AIU ARWI ZRYY ?

VIC
HUA
XXX